POLAND'S WAR CALCULATION 1939

By Stefan Scheil

Poland's Reasons, Hopes and Aims in 1939 - Get a new view on the origins of the war between Poland and Germany which eventually became World War II

Poland's War Calculation in1939

Reasons, Hopes and Aims

By

Stefan Scheil

3

"Heathen land is no-man's land. In this case, who owns today the German land which claims to be neo-heathen? Would Reichsleiter Rosenberg be able to provide a perfectly honest answer?"

Józef Kisielewski (From: The Earth saves the bygone days, 1939)[1]

"After the upcoming war ..., Poland should annex Danzig, East Prussia, Upper and Central Silesia including Breslau, and Central Pomerania including Kolberg; furthermore, Poland should set up under her protection and leadership a number of buffer states along the Oder and Neisse rivers."

Jedrzej Giertych (From a newspaper article, summer of 1939)[2]

---

[1] Quoted from Kisielewski, Earth, p. 97 et seq. Józef Kisielewski (1906–1966) was a Polish journalist, writer and politician.

[2] Quoted from Giertych, Pol wieku poslkiej polityki, p. 180 et seq. Giertych (1903-1992), in 1939, was a member of the Central Committee of the National Democratic Party and the founder of a minor political dynasty. His grandson, Roman Giertych was assistant head of state of the Polish Republic until 2007.

4

Herstellung und Verlag:
BoD - Books on Demand, Norderstedt
ISBN 978-3-7448-2257-2

5

Table of Contents

Introduction

Let us begin with a clarification of the terms used in this book. Poland's war calculations of 1939 were part of the consequences of Poland's fight for its rebirth as a state, for its borders and for its establishment on the international stage. This fight went on incessantly in the years between 1918 and 1939, initially, more often than not, as a Hot War, with interspersed Cold War phases; occasionally, there even appeared to be phases of détente with respect to neighboring countries.

Still, for Poland, these never-ending disputes took on an existential significance, because the right to exist as a political entity in the shape envisioned by Poland at its recreation in 1918 did not go without opposition. Poland claimed sovereignty over other peoples and ethnic groups. These claims collided with the principles behind the international standard of "self-determination of nations" that had just been proclaimed in 1919; on a more practical level it also clashed with a long list of political interests of other states. The Polish empire in the inter-war years was an anachronism.

The conflict with Lithuania, another country that had been put (back) on the map at the end of the First World War, is a case in point. It concerned the city of Vilnius (Wilna) and turned out to be the only such case which Poland, in 1938, was able to bring to a successful end without outside help. No such successes were achieved in other cases under dispute. Polish claims for the Ukraine and White Russia were rejected by the Soviet Union, a state which Warsaw did not even recognize. Polish agencies were working towards the dissolution of these states under the label of "Prometheism" and were confident that the break-up take would place before the end of the Second World War.[3] By the criteria of international law and from the point of view of domination over other ethnic groups, Polish-German relations were particularly explosive. The aims and actions of the Polish republic in respect of the German state and the ethnic Germans in Poland were clearly at odds with

---

[3] In November 1943 the Polish foreign ministry, in a memorandum, requested the dissolution of Russia as well as the extension of Poland toward the east beyond the pre-war borders. "We make no hasty claims for a break-up of Russia , but if such possibilities should arise we support the independence of the Ukraine and the Caucasian Federation. We strive for the transformation of the all-Russian empire into national states ... . In the east, in case of a transformation of Russia, we desire a rounding-off including Kamieniec and Minsk. Lithuania must form a unified state with Poland, in which case we are ready to confer complete equality of rights to the Lithuanians. Furthermore, we are eying minute border corrections concerning Romania and possibly Latvia." Quoted after Gelberg, Entstehung, p. 36.

the right to self-determination and were inacceptable for any German government.

This latter problem became decisive in 1939. This is not to mean that Poland eventually bore the unique responsibility for the German-Polish war of 1939 or for other wars. In an era of world wars, there are no unique causes. Any such explanation would be inadmissibly deficient. The present book does try, however, to retrace the road to war from the Polish point of view. When Poland opted for a confrontational course with respect to its German neighbor in early 1939, she did have certain ideas. Long envisioned aims were to be realized by this step.

As we shall see, the intellectual roots of these aims reached back far into the 19th century. A fight with Germany for a Polish expansion westward, up to the Oder river and northward, up to the coast of the Baltic Sea, a fight for territories that, at some time in history had been or were alleged to have been Polish lands in Pomerania, Silesia, and Brandenburg, was an objective that had been conjured up as inevitable by numerous Polish authors over many decades.

Among them we have poets and intellectuals, historians and geographers and, last not least, politicians and soldiers. The year 1939 was thought to be favorable for such a battle because the international constellation looked promising. From a Polish point of view, such an assessment was realistic and understandable. Therefore, up to the coast of the Baltic Sea, a fight for territories that, at some time in history had been or were alleged to have been Polish lands in Pomerania, Silesia, and Brandenburg, was an objective that had been conjured up as inevitable by numerous Polish authors over many decades.

Over the last so many decades, much has been written about Polish and German ideas in respect of the disputed areas; Poland's expansionist plans have been clearly demonstrated, yet this has in no way altered the thesis that on 1st September 1939, Germany launched a surprise attack on Poland. In the minds of authors dealing with contemporary history, there are no Polish plans preceding the above date – a completely erroneous position, to say the least.

In Germany, the Polish assessment faced fundamental anti-Polish opinions and tendencies. Poland had every right to fear for her very existence. In the early Weimar republic, no German chancellor or politician worth his salt, was in any way inclined to respect Germany's eastern border which the Germans had been forced, literally at gunpoint, to accept at Versailles. It went without saying that they strove for a readjustment of the border with Poland, but they also questioned the very legal and practical bases of Poland's existence as an independent state.

Both Gustav Stresemann and Joseph Wirth, German chancellors, subscribed to a policy of "Poloniam esse delendam". The head of the Reichswehr, General Seeckt, considered the existence of Poland to be "incompatible with German interests". Bernhard von Bülow, long-time Chief Secretary of the German Foreign Office and certainly no National Socialist, demanded "one last partition of Poland". Significant segments of the German political scene had thus not yet accepted the existence of the new state of Poland and considered it to be the very symbol of the German defeat in 1918. We will not elaborate on this point, its aspects are well-known.

What is less well-known, on the other hand, are Poland's own expansionist plans. This is quite surprising, as they were just as fundamental in their scope as those of the Germans. It is true that only a few lines of thought went so far as to deny the Germans – be they Germanic or simply across the board – the right to exist to the south of Denmark. However, when we come to the advancement of the Polish border far into central Germany, or the displacement of the German capital from Berlin to Frankfurt on the Main, or the carving up of Germany into a desirable number of smaller states, there is no shortage of radical utterances by famous and influential Polish personalities.

In the text which follows, we shall describe briefly the ideas then 'en vogue' on the Polish side and their effects on Warsaw's political decisions in the period before the outbreak of hostilities in 1939. We realize that this is a delicate subject and can easily be misinterpreted. The author published, in June 2006, a lengthy article in the Frankfurter Allgemeine Zeitung, entitled "Central European visions of power after Versailles" and describing the Polish political considerations. It provoked a rebuttal by Gesine Schwan, at the time president of the "Europa-Universität Viadrina" at Frankfurt on Oder, who, in a lecture at the German Historical Institute in Washington, D.C., maintained that Scheil, an independent historian, had described the German "Drang nach Osten" as a mere reaction to a Polish "Drang nach Westen".[4] This was never stated nor intended as an interpretation. The essential thesis was: In the spring of 1939, the Polish government took a conscious decision. It decided to launch the long-expected conflict with Germany within the year. The present booklet attempts to describe, from the perspective of the Warsaw government, the assumptions on which the decision rested and the ensuing events. Quite obviously, there exist

---

[4]http://www.ghidc.org/files/publications/bulletin/bu040/039.pdf, p. 46.

many other ways of describing the events of 1939; in this case, we have chosen to examine the Polish point of view.

The Basis: the new Polish nationalism

An analysis of the colonial history of various parts of the world has shown that the evolution of colonized countries, i.e. countries that came under foreign domination, can often be subdivided into a number of clearly distinguishable phases with respect to the concentration of political power. This refers both to the leading personalities and to the ideological contents. Initially, we have the traditional ruling classes, i.e. the established monarchs, the nobility or, at times, the religious leaders, that are disenfranchised by the invaders to the point where they and the country itself lose their sovereignty.

Once the colonial power has installed itself, revolts or other types of resistance are still basically led by the indigenous elite. Over the course of time, however, lack of success and changes in the social structure will cause the rise of new political parties which will fight the foreign domination under entirely different political or ideological banners.

In the case of Poland which had ceased to be a state as a consequence of the three partitions of the country between 1772 and 1795 and had become a region considered to be a colony by the new overlords, the second phase of the evolution described above came to an end in January, 1863, with the failure of the third armed uprising against the Russian domination. This renewed defeat clearly showed that individual uprisings against the three ruling powers, Prussia, Austro-Hungary, and Russia in particular, were doomed to fail. At the same time, a new kind of Polish nationalism took hold, initially in a pre-political sphere – e.g. at the universities and in literature – tending to question not only the concept of Polish greatness and the Polish past, but also to examine the causes of the national disaster.

As early as the beginning of the 19th century, Polish authors conjured up the alleged Slavic past of much of the territory of the German Confederation as it existed at the time. Similar ideas were increasingly entertained by the "Pan-Slavic movement" which was formally founded in Prague in 1848 by the "Pan-Slavic Congress". Other political groupings and authors adopted requests for the establishment of a future Polish state which was to extend westward up to the Oder estuary.[5] These objectives became very popular, to the point that, as early as 1860, Karl Marx formulated a diatribe:

> *"For Vogt, the Russian panslavist, who already rules Bohemia, there can be no question as to the line of the natural border*

---

[5] Cf. Gehrke, Westgedanke, p. 64 et seq.

of the Slavic empire. Starting out from Meseritz, it runs directly towards Lieberose, then south from the passage of the Elbe river through the Bohemian border country and then follows the western and southern border of Bohemia and Moravia. What lies to the east, is Slavic, those few German enclaves and other intrusions into Slavic territory will not stand up to the re-establishment of the Slavic whole; in any case, they have no right to be where they are.

Once this 'pan-Slavic entity' has come into its own, it goes without saying that, to the south, a similar rectification of the borders will impose itself. We Germans will lose nothing in the process – except East and West Prussia, Silesia, parts of Brandenburg and Saxony, all of Bohemia, Moravia and the remainder of Austria, except for Tyrol (part of which will be subjected to the Italian 'Nationalitätsprinzip' (principle of nationality) – and will throw our national existence into the bargain!"[6]

This pan-Slavic movement played a major part in the definition of Polish nationalism. On the other hand, the discussion of these ideas and their adoption by Russian intellectuals and politicians, eventually led to a differentiation.

---

[6] Quoted from Marx, Vogt, p. 130 et seq.

While the range of Slavic demands was basically similar, many masterminds of Polish nationalism refused to accept Russian leadership of a pan-Slavistic state. Their aim was Polish independence after a successful war against Germany. This sometimes led to surprising alliances and would, in the long run, eventually take on truly prophetic traits. An anonymous author, writing under the pen-name of "Der Slawe" (the Slav) in 1872, formally declared a "racial war" between the Germans and the Slavs. He was hoping for an all-Slavic conquest of the lands east of the Oder river, or, better still, east of the Elbe.

Once that would have been accomplished, the Russian Tsar would realize that Polish independence within these borders would be in his own interest.[7] Other authors stood back from such Polish-Russian alliances because of the Russification which St. Petersburg began to practice after the failed uprising of 1863, which went so far as to prohibit the use of Latin script (normally used in writing Polish) in print. The culmination was the erection of a gigantic orthodox cathedral in Warsaw, which – being a symbol of past oppression – would be promptly torn down completely when a catholic Poland came into her own once again in 1919.[8]

---

[7] Cf. Un Slave, Geneva 1872, p. 17 et seq., also Gehrke, Westgedanke, p. 97.
[8] This refers to the Alexander-Nevski-Cathedral. The location was renamed "Independence Square".

Around the turn of the century, reflecting these tendencies, a call for general Polish leadership in Central Europe became one of the main characteristics of the nascent Polish nationalism; it would compete with Russian hegemony, not only within Poland. For the Polish national movement it was not only a matter of re-establishing the political sovereignty of the Polish people under the auspices of "national self-determination". On this point, there was widespread agreement between the otherwise widely differing political camps. Of late, the Polish historian Marek Kornat has succinctly stated the matter thus: "But the Polish people would not subscribe to the concept of an 'ethnic Poland'".[9]

Rather, such as in the mind of Josef Pilsudski, the aim was to be the task of a renewed civilizing mission in Eastern Europe, together with a considerable revision of the German-Polish border in the West, ultimately on the basis of conditions obtaining in the Middle Ages. With such imperial aspirations, Poland came back on the map of Europe in 1918 and would pursue these ideas until 1939, both on a national and an international level. In an era dominated in Europe by the slogan of "self-determination of peoples" such a policy could not be promulgated on the international scene.

---

[9] Cf. Kornat, Polen, p.27. The author is a professor at the Historical Institute of the Polish Academy of Sciences.

Hence, between 1919 and 1939, Poland had to pursue a quiet line which, fundamentally, went against international law; she largely succeeded in hiding her basic policy from becoming known in the Western capitals.

In the political debate, the term "kresy" acquired an enlarged meaning. Originally, it designated the "stolen territories" in the east which, after 1815, no longer belonged to the "Kingdom of Poland" ruled by the Russians, but had been fully integrated into Russia itself, such as the western part of the Ukraine as we know it today. From about 1900 onwards, the word "kresy" was applied to western lands as well. In the words of Jan Ludwik Poplawski, one of the masterminds of Polish thought at the time, the term was defined as follows:

"We designate as borderlands [i.e. kresy] those provinces which comprise significant Polish minorities, both indigenous and immigrated, but also the ethnographically Polish regions the populations of which are not nationally conscious in the political sense. This refers to the provinces which either were never part of the Polish state [sic] or which separated themselves from it ages ago, but also [the regions] in which the political and cultural domination of the

Polish element has been seriously upset and weakened".[10]

This definition thus englobed all territories which could be construed as having been "Slavic" and hence "ethnographically Polish" – in prehistoric or protohistoric times. It referred i.a. to East Prussia – which was alleged to possess a Slavic past – and to Silesia. Finally, Pomerania, Mecklenburg, Brandenburg and large parts of Saxony or Saxony-Anhalt, were also claimed in this manner. Historical or present-day facts regarding the true presence of a Slavic-Polish population or the actual constitutional past were of little importance. Any Germans present in these areas represented "Zaborczosc" [conquest] and were thus guilty of greed for alien, Slavic property.

This concept, too, became popular after 1900 and was, in a way, the mirror image of the German view of having acted as "harbingers of culture" in the East. Polish "Western studies" which had had their place before 1914, primarily at Austrian universities, were better organized and promoted after 1918, primarily at the University of Posen; it produced pseudo-scientific arguments for all comers. Real political manifestations of the local population

---

[10] Quoted from Popławski, Grenzmarken, p. 672. On the subject of the meaning of
"Kresy" cf. Gehrke, Westgedanke, p. 19 et seq.

in the disputed territories were insignificant in the internal Polish dialog.

Even a plebiscite in the southern part of East Prussia, controlled by the victorious powers, which resulted in a vote of not less than 97.9 percent for Germany (probably a world record for this kind of plebiscite) did not keep the Polish government from lodging a formal protest. It criticized as unclear the labelling of the ballots and caused a long drawn-out political campaign on the Polish side which claimed that the South of East Prussia was Polish nonetheless.

Under these conditions, the Polish uprising of 1918 turned into an immediate and uncompromising attack on anything German in the regions demanded by Poland. In the city and province of Posen, (Polish: Poznan) Polish forces not only confiscated weapons and took over the administration but also started to remove all German symbols and monuments. Wherever there was German military resistance, the German population was expelled on the spot.[11] The Germans in the western regions of the nascent Polish republic, in particular, were considered to be an irremediable danger for the stability of the new state.

---

[11] Cf. Blanke, Orphans, p. 15 et seq.

It was assumed by the Polish authorities – and probably rightly so - that they would never give up their demands for a reintegration into a German state. But beyond such suspicions, the program of the permanent revolt against the political, social and economic development, as it had been mapped out by the Polish nationalists over the two preceding centuries, simply denied the Germans the right of residence in the republic. They would have to leave the country. Stanislaw Grabski, the president of the committee of foreign relations in the Sejm, the "province of Posen demonstrates how the presence of foreigners in the country can be brought down from fourteen or even twenty percent to one and a half percent … Polish land for the Poles!"[12]

The "foreigners, in this case, were the Germans. Later on, Grabski went even further and spoke of the Polish character of East Prussia and of an unavoidable battle with Germany, which would have to be won to allow further expansion towards the coast of the Baltic Sea. Such views were not the exception and were uttered on the government level as well. In a widely noted statement, the prime minister Wladyslaw Sikorski urged explicitly to move ahead with the "de-Germanization" by all available means. A good tool, in this case, would be the expropriation of German property and the

---

[12] As stated by Stanislaw Grabski in his political program of 1919, quoted here from Blanke, Orphans, p. 63.

dismissal of German workers and employees as this would do away with the material basis of German life.

Together with the closure of German schools and a general "Kulturkampf" (cultural battle) these measures would achieve the desired result. Polish national feeling in the post-war years was impregnated with the conviction that the history of the preceding centuries would have to be complete revised. Political, economic and ethnic conditions as they existed within or outside of Poland would have to be discarded. Poland would have to be recreated.

Europe's seminal catastrophe seen as an opportunity – the First World War from the Polish point of view

It is well known that the history of the recreated Polish state did not begin in 1918. The First World War enabled the Poles who lived in the tsarist empire, i.e. in "Congress Poland", to enjoy certain state-like structures. For the German-Polish relations, the period between 1915 and 1918 in a way heralded what was to come. German indecision on whether Polish independence was desirable or not - and if so, within what limits – became apparent.

At the same time, and quite apart from German ideas and the prevailing political situation, Polish insistence on a future state which would comprise significant parts of the German Reich was brought to the fore. Whereas in the rest of Europe where nations, after initial enthusiasm for the war, began to realize how much they stood to lose, the Polish national movement saw the war as a godsend. For half a century, a Polish state had been seen as something which could only rise again from the ashes of a war.

Under the weight of the Russian occupation, certain structures of an underground state had already come into being. For a while, they could be distinguished in the 1912 boycott of Jewish tradesmen. Only two years later, the war began and Polish independence became palpable. Armed forces had to be formed. As early as August 1914, a Polish legion, commanded by Josef Pilsudski, the future dictator, moved into battle. The initial fight against Russia, so Pilsudski said, would eventually be directed against Germany.

This attitude became a model for Poland in the inter-war years, and the date, the "Day of the Legion", would be commemorated yearly with great pomp and circumstance. On 6 August 1939, the twenty-fifth anniversary of the event, particularly threatening speeches were directed towards Germany. Four days later, in Berlin, the Polish ministry of foreign affairs threatened Germany openly with an attack.[13]

In any case, in August 1915, the German forces succeeded in taking Warsaw and in keeping the Russian army out of Congress Poland for the three years to come. This success resulted in a German-Austrian military administration for the conquered territory and its inhabitants. Initially, no particular political concept went along with this move although early into the war, there had been speculations in Germany in respect of the Polish calls for independence.

---

[13] The German government was informed, that any future letters concerning Danzig would be regarded as an attack with the corresponding consequences. Cf. White Book of the Polish government, document 86, 10 August 1939.

Leaflets in Polish, in the first weeks of the conflict, stated that the German and Austrian forces would bring Polish "Freedom and Independence".[14] Within a short time, though, "Congress Poland" became a problem, involving not only Polish but also Ukrainian, White Russian, Lithuanian, and Jewish interests, to say nothing of the ideas of the indigenous German minority.

Obviously, divergent political interests within the individual ethnicities made the matter yet more complex, and the generally somewhat difficult relationship between the Germans and the Austrians did not help. For administrative reasons, Congress Poland had been divided into two zones of occupation, the Government General of Warsaw, on the German side, and the Lublin area administrated by Austria. Under the circumstances, it was hardly possible to elaborate a common administration or unified concept for Poland. Still, numerous measures, aimed at a cultural and political rebirth of Poland, were undertaken. Passports bearing the entry "Polish citizen" were issued, Polish universities were created, Russian place names were replaced by Polish designations and free elections for municipal councils in the occupied territories were instituted.

---

[14] Cf. Roth, Kongreßpolen, p. 18.

Nonetheless, as soon as the Warsaw municipal council had met for its first session, it became clear that this was not enough. The city demanded "an independent Polish state, with the necessary bodies and means to assure its independence – that is the highest aim of previous and present endeavors of the Polish nation. This is also our most holy aim which we strive for." A national-democratic brochure of 1916 described Germany and Austria facing an insoluble problem as far as the question of independence was concerned and stated ironically:

"Our position in the face of the Germanic states is difficult, but we have to admit that the position of the Germanic states with respect to the Polish question is deplorable. They cannot give us our independence, they cannot produce a unified state from the whole Polish territory, and they have yet to resolve the quandary they are in: to obtain Poland's unshakable friendship while, at the same time, neglecting the old rights of the Polish people".[15]

---

[15] From the brochure of the National Democratic Party, "Von Jasna Gora nach Hellberg", summer 1916, quoted here from Roth, Kongreßpolen, p. 38. The accuracy of this viewpoint is confirmed by Josef Neumann's brochure "Beiträge zur Lösung der polnischen Frage" (contributions for the resolution of the Polish question), also dated 1916. Most of these German texts aimed for the separation of Poland from Russia under German

A vital point of the movement for independence was the existence of an armed force which, however, would be placed at the disposal of the potential allies only under certain conditions. Within the months following the declaration of the Warsaw council, a request for the creation of a Polish army was repeatedly addressed to the Central Powers, Germany and Austro-Hungary. The proclamation of a Polish state and the creation of a Polish army were to take place simultaneously.

This also entailed the transfer of the administration into Polish hands, a condition which was subscribed to by all political parties interested in such a proclamation. It was not to be fulfilled. Eventually, on 5 November 1916, the Central Powers proclaimed a Kingdom of Poland without a head of state, without clearly defined borders, without an independent army and without its own administration, which was to "develop its powers freely" in combination [im Anschluss] with Germany and Austria.

It is not surprising that hardly anyone would join the armed forces under these conditions; recruiting campaigns by German offices remained ineffective. Still, this brought the Polish questions onto the international agenda

---

control by some kind of semi-national dependence. Full independence was considered impossible in view of Polish expansionist aims towards Danzig and Posen, seen as inevitable. Cf. Neumann, Beiträge, passim.

and was thus a considerable achievement for the Polish national movement. The reactions of Polish politicians within the occupied territory were positive, at least officially. The Polish members of the Russian parliament were unhappy and announced on this occasion what they really aimed for, as for example the national democrat Harusewicz:

> *"We object decidedly against this German act which confirms the Polish partition and seeks to prevent the need for a Polish unification. Such a unification is impossible without Cracow, Posen, Silesia and the Polish Sea".* [16]

Taken together, this amounted to territorial demands up to the Oder-Neisse line. The demands for German territory were considerable and resulted from decades of political agitation which had reached a stage where any political concessions would only have brought along further demands. Even Josef Pilsudski who appeared to be an ally of the Central Powers wanted Polish independence and large tracts of land that were German territories. His program required the simultaneous defeat of both Germany and Russia. Hence, the German dilemma mentioned above truly existed, because the Polish requests could not be accepted by any kind of German government. At the same time, this aims were made public in Western Europe as well. A

---

[16] Quoted from Roth, Kongreßpolen, p. 44.

"Polish Information Committee" promoted a future Polish empire abroad. In 1917, the respected London publishing house Allen & Unwin printed of pamphlet of this organization which called for a Polish Empire stretching from Berlin to the suburbs of Moscow.

The first Russian revolution in February 1917 and the continuing advance of German troops produced further problems for which Polish and German political solutions were mutually exclusive. Berlin intended to bring about the independence of both the Baltic countries and especially the Ukraine; Germany achieved these aims in a treaty with the nascent USSR in early 1918 and thereby collided with Poland in regions which Polish nationalism considered to be Polish home ground. At the same time, the Entente also placed the Polish question on their political agenda.

On 3 June 1918, they announced that "the creation of a unified and independent Polish state with free access to the sea" was one of their conditions for peace – the Polish political agitation in the West had thus yielded a positive result. This agitation had, for many years, involved the help of such famous personalities as the pianist Ignaz Paderewski or the national democrat Roman Dmowski, as well as persons less well known today like the Philosopher Wincenty Lutoslawski who, as early as the turn of the century, had produced a map on which large parts of Germany and Russia were part of a new Poland which he presented on lecture tours in the USA. This brought about direct political consequences both in the USA and in Europe. The persons mentioned would all be members of the Polish delegation to the Versailles peace conference.

By the most devious and grotesque means, this delegation attempted to cause the victorious powers to confer large parts of Germany to Poland. One of the brochures which were presented at the conference was entitled "Danzig and East Prussia". In line with the electoral constitution for the Sejm, elaborated in November 1918, both territories were to become Polish.[17] To reinforce this demand, a fictitious "Mazurian Mission" was invented which was said to have travelled to Warsaw in March 1919 in order to request the local inter-allied mission for the integration of Mazuria into Poland.[18] This delegation allegedly represented the people, but the people were not to be consulted.

If, however, the Allies were to hold a plebiscite in this region, this could only be done after the "elimination of German officials, clergymen

---

[17] This electoral decree also comprised all of Silesia up to the eastern Neisse river, all of West Prussia, southern East Prussia and parts of Pomerania. Cf. Lauen, Zwischenspiel, p. 14.

[18] Cf. Lutoslawski, Gdansk, p. 29.

and soldiers"; a (Polish) occupation over so many years was necessary to achieve this. Elsewhere, the pamphlet mentioned German "parasites" in Mazuria who had to be removed.[19] The logic of this policy of eradication would bear fruit in 1945, when the Mazurians, considered to be unfit for integration into Poland were expulsed into what remained of Germany; the idea was clearly apparent in the last sentence of the brochure, which read:

> *"It would be most unfair to Poland to hold a plebiscite in a province as Polish as Mazuria before the Mazurian have emancipated themselves fully from any kind of German influence and this can only be achieved through its reunification with Poland."[20]*

This passage proves that any kind of success in a plebiscite could only be achieved through a mixture of force, expulsion and re-education under Polish domination. Still, the Allies opted for a number of plebiscites which took place in the regions in southern East Prussia just mentioned and in Upper Silesia. In all cases, clear majorities in favor of Germany resulted. Even though the Polish side attempted to create facts by means of armed infringements, especially in Upper Silesia, this method was only partly successful.

---

[19] Cf. Lutoslawski, Gdansk, p. 35.
[20] Quoted from Lutoslawski, Gdansk, p. 32.

Poland was neither able to break armed German resistance by herself, nor could democratically legitimate majorities be obtained for the Polish cause. In the end, further westward expansion depended on the good will of the western powers. Josef Pilsudski, by now a legendary leader of the Polish legions and future dictator, summed things up as follows: "For the moment, Poland has no borders. Anything we can do in the West depends on the Entente, on whether it is ready to compress Germany further or less so". That is the way it would stay. Without an international coalition, Poland could achieve little against Germany.

Poland's phantom dilemma after 1919: Empire or failure

"Striving to become a major power was the curse of our political line… Polish power politics did not relinquish concepts for the separation of the Ukraine and the Caucasus from Russia and carried on with the objective of absorbing Danzig or even East Prussia. Certain activities in this direction, which can best be described as walking on egg shells, were for all intents and purposes undertaken by state agencies or by institutions financed by the national budget. The public was unbelievably proud of this and very satisfied with the matter".

Michal Lubienski, cabinet chief of the Polish foreign minister.[21]

In view of the fact that, for the moment, nothing could be done against Germany, Pilsudski, instead of moving west turned east, towards the USSR. Attempts have been made to depict this war as a preventive measure against aggressive Soviet plans. Actually, however, the Soviets were still deeply involved in the Russian civil war and would have been hard put to carry out

---

[21] Notes from 1940/41, quoted here from Łubienski, Polen, p. 79.

offensive actions. During his campaign in the East, Pilsudski even helped them against internal Russian enemies such as General Denikin whom he rightly suspected of harboring ambitions for a Greater Russia, which were incompatible with his own dreams of a Polish-Lithuanian-Ukrainian federation. As against this, the Polish partitions and the results of the Vienna Congress also figured on a comprehensive list of earlier international agreements prepared by the Soviets which they were no longer ready to respect.

This was a highly significant contribution to the Polish position; moreover, Pilsudski was repeatedly offered, in March 1919, a Polish-Russian border based on the conditions obtaining in 1772. Still, the answer was no. Pilsudski believed himself to be militarily superior and envisaged raising Poland to the level of "the greatest powers of the world", as he had publicly announced in January 1920. The 1772 border, with Kiev as a frontier city, would no longer have been useful for such a plan.

Kiev was to be the center of a Greater Ukraine, a Polish satellite. This had been the case in the 17th century and the assertion of not being satisfied with "1772" was a recurrent element of Polish politics and Polish publications in the interwar period. Over the years, the competing plans, such as Roman Dmowski's idea of moving west, primarily against Germany, began to melt with Pilsudski's imperial visions. The government of the 1930s was, after all, solidly in the hands of the Pilsudskites who, for the most part, shared common memories of their life as veterans of the Polish legion in the First World War and thus formed a rather closed and secretive entity.

Nonetheless, the attempt actually to occupy the Ukraine in 1920 became a failure. While Polish troops did advance as far as Kiev, they were unable to hold on to the lands they had conquered. French support enabled Poland to save itself, but only parts of the Ukraine and White Russia were ceded to Poland in the ensuing "Peace of Riga".

This was not enough to fulfill her ambitions. The borders of Central Europe remained entirely tentative, not only from Warsaw's point of view. At the same time, throughout the 1920s, Poland had also to face flexible German political moves which resulted in making the world conscious of the loss of West Prussia and the "Corridor problem". The German foreign office was to sign no further agreement with Poland recognizing the Versailles borders. Occasionally, the Polish republic found itself in a defensive position which, however, was countered on the international scene. Within Poland, these moves were reinforced by a whole array of measures aimed at making life in Poland impossible for the local ethnic Germans.

Brutal force became the order of the day, just like the dismissal of German workers and employees, a silent expropriation by the introduction of a Polish pre-emptive right applicable to successions or the closure of German schools. Some other states were outspoken admirers of such policies and devised measures of their own for future use. Some of his Counselors, for example, advised the Czech-Slovakian president Benes to imitate the Poles who had shown the way by "throwing out" one and a half million Germans. On the other hand, the advice that Poland should "do three million of them in, like in a slaughter-house" would not be heeded. Murder was to be discarded in favor of re-education.[22]

In the end, Pilsudski's project of a Polish empire resulting directly from the First World War remained unaccomplished. The slogan of an "Intermarium", a Polish state ranging from the Black Sea to the Baltic, remained a vision which would continue to occupy his successors. Polish access to the sea remained limited to the narrow coastal strip of West Prussia, once Lithuania would not go along with Polish claims for leadership. While Pilsudski did occupy the city of Wilna, Lithuania's projected

---

[22] E.g. Bretislaw Palkovsky in a letter to Benes, dated 7 November 1940. Cf. Brandes, Weg, p. 84.

capital, he advanced no further. Poland was unable to pocket the strip of German land around the city of Memel, the Memelland, which the Allies had simply cut off without even asking the local population, intending to present it to the projected Polish-Lithuanian Union as a port and a passageway.

In the end, it would be occupied by Lithuania. The republic of Poland went on to remain a state which almost everywhere extended beyond ethnically Polish areas, to the point where Poles retained a tenuous majority in the country.

In spite of her military and political achievements, the new Poland had scored poorly. The call for the former borders of the Polish monarchy, vaguely defensible in an era of dynastically governed, but multi-ethnic states, was rather out of place in postwar Europe and its superheated nationalistic atmosphere; it tagged the whole Polish enterprise as something anachronistic.

For Poland, at the end of the 1920s, there were only two borders that were recognized by both sides: the border with Romania and the one with Latvia. Thus, Warsaw politics had to be content with the vision of being able to revive former glory and concentrate on anything that could be claimed on the basis of even the faintest historical rights. Far-reaching demands were raised against Lithuania and Czechoslovakia, territorial transfer demands were expected from Germany and Russia while Poland was even unhappy with her own possessions.

It is impossible, within the scope of this work, to display in detail the many radical utterances by Polish media and politicians with respect to claims against Germany. A typical example would be a memorandum of the Polish foreign ministry of 1931 which mentioned the Oder-Neisse line as the ultimate aim of Polish expansion.[23]24 Such ideas enjoyed great popularity nationwide, also in military circles. A book written in 1927 by Henryk Baginski, a member of the Polish general staff in which such ideas were brought to the attention of the public enjoyed several editions. It contained such statements as:

> *"There will never be peace in Europe until Prussia has been erased and the German capital moved from Berlin to Frankfurt on the Main, as Berlin is located on Slavic land. Only a revision of the Slavic defeat will ensure the suppression of Germany."[24]*

The interesting aspect of this matter was the career of the author who was moved to the general staff and remained there until 1939 only

---

[23] According to Kurt Gräbe, ethnic German member of the Polish parliament between 1922 and 1936, member of its foreing affairs committee in 1931. Cf. Neumeyer, Westpreußen, p. 400.

[24] Quoted from Baginski, Poland, p. 86.

after he had publicly demanded the occupation of East Prussia and the displacement of the German capital.[25] To name an officer with such aggressive views to the general staff in the years before the war was an unmistakable signal. Furthermore, it should be noted that Baginski had raised his demands on the basis of the theory of the "Third Europe" or the "Intermarium". This theory held that in the way France linked the Atlantic and the Mediterranean and Germany the North Sea and the Adriatic, Poland should serve as a link between the Baltic and the Black Sea.[26] Thus, Polish territorial demands were well defined, all the more so as the Oder estuary was generally taken to be the western end of this link, also by Baginski. Baginski's book, "Poland's Freedom of the Sea", in the English edition of 1942, went further yet when it called the Elbe a "great Slavic river" and provided a map which placed Poland's "historical borders" just east of the city of Brunswick.[27] He was perhaps too modest

---

[25] Marian Kukiel in the foreword to the book "Poland's Freedom of the Sea", underlines that Baginski had been one of the men who , in the years before the war, had laid the foundation for the future armed forces of Poland. Cf. Baginski, Freedom p. III.

[26] Cf. Baginski, Freedom, p. 10 et seq., and Scheil, Logik, p. 106 et seq.

[27] Cf. Baginski, Freedom, p. 28, map 6. It can be seen that, from this point of view, practically the whole territory that would later be the Soviet zone of occupation of Germany was "historically" part of Poland. This also held for all of the Ukraine, for Russia up to Borodino, i.e.

to go as far as to call the Rhine as a Slavic waterway. but indicated that this would have been justified in the light of his general argument: because "two thousand five hundred years ago, the better part of today's Germany up to the Rhine was settled by Slavs".[28]

Similar assertions of sectors of the Polish press to the effect that the population of the lands east of the Oder-Neisse line were fundamentally indigenous Slavs who had simply been superficially Germanized and that the small remainder represented by actual Germans or "stubborn Germanized Slavs" could simply be sent back to where they had come from,[29] add up to a nationalistic and racial program of

up to a point some 100 km to the west of Moscow. The whole of the Baltic states except for a small strip of land around the Estonian capital Reval shared the same fate.

[28] Quoted after Baginski, Freedom, p.29. Here, Baginski links up with the theories of the well-known Polish historian Wojciech Ketrzynski (1838–1918) who had stated that all of "Germania" was inhabited by Poles at the time of Julius Caesar; e.g. the Suevi were said to be a Slavic tribe. Such theories enabled Ketrzynski to become – in the tolerant Austro-Hungarian state - director of the Lemberg (Today: Lwow) Library and to be fondly remembered by the Polish national movement. Cf. Gehrke, Westgedanke, p. 131.

[29] Polish media at the time computed a Polish share of up to 75% for the German population east of the Elbe. The record holder in this respect was apparently Edward Boguslawski, who claimed, as early as 1912, that this applied to the German population as such (!). Cf. Boguslawski, Gebiete, quoted here as per Baginski, Freedom, S. 71.

territorial expansion, never before encountered in European history. Some ten million inhabitants of an area covering more than forty thousand square miles of land would be told that their existence was based upon a mistake and had to be terminated –either by expulsion or by a reversion to a mystical "Polish identity" that their forebears had allegedly possessed hundreds of years earlier:

> *"If the Irish can revert to their Celtic tradition and language, if the Jews in Palestine can become Hebrews once more, there is no reason why the population east of the Elbe cannot revert to their Slavic tradition. Viewed as a whole, the Polonization of the "Half-Germans" would be much less dangerous for Europe than the Germanization of Poland and would, moreover, be in line with the historical trend as Slavs have a higher vitality".[30]*

Even on the European scene of the nationalistic period there is no comparable claim in any nationalistic program. Polish "Western thoughts" for a long time remained on a singular level, until the Czech policy started to beget similar ideas. By comparison, the German-French squabble about Alsace-Lorraine was harmless and conventional. In that case, no side undertook any measures of ethnic cleansing or even entertained such ideas, in

---

[30] Quoted as per Baginski, Freedom, p. 71 et seq.

spite of all their differences. As opposed to this, the German-Polish conflict of 1939 in its brutal fundamentality had a long history which should show its ugly face in the days just before and after the outbreak of the hostilities; members of the German minority in Poland would be murdered and the German retaliation would be no less ugly.

For the moment though, Poland had its ambitions and wanted to be a major power, but emerged from the unrest of the post-war years as a mere guarantor of the results of Versailles and as the main partner for France in Eastern Europe. Pilsudski retired from politics in 1923 for several years. After the end of the French occupation of the Ruhr and the acceptance of the Dawes plan by Germany, Europe entered a period of rest which left no room for "power politics" aimed at readjustments of borders or new military alliances. The confusing internal affairs in Poland prevented the development of any entity which would have been strong enough to carry out a policy of expansion. This state would come to an end only when, in 1926, Pilsudski returned as a major figure and when the German question resurfaced in the early 1930s.

In the long run, the attempt to repair, in the 20th century, the failings of the Polish state two hundred years earlier, backfired in two ways: on the one hand, Polish activities in the 1930s contributed decisively to the destabilization of Eastern Europe. Much too big and much too weak, as it then was, Poland would once again be partitioned, something that would have been difficult to imagine if the country had been satisfied with ethnically justifiable borders earlier on. Secondly, the self-created dilemma of imperial aspirations cleared the way for Poland's own annihilation.

These aspirations could not be sold to the outside world and led the country into isolation. Unfortunately, only a few people in Warsaw saw things in this way. For the moment, the return of the German question brought up the specter of a European crisis. The Pilsudskites regarded this as a chance, in the way the First World War had been a chance. Now it was a matter of assembling an international constellation for this chance to be used in the best possible way.

Poland's war calculation - The necessary international constellation

Since 1919, nothing had changed in the way Poland viewed possible moves against Germany. For Pilsudski, the question had been to what degree the Entente powers, basically France and Britain, were ready to "compress" Germany. At the same time, the East had to be clear, i.e. there should be no risk of a Soviet attack. Pilsudski never made a secret of his intention to act militarily against both the Weimar republic and the early National Socialism, as he repeatedly told London and Paris, "twice a year" as Robert Vansittart, long-time chief of the British Foreign Office, noted somewhat derisively later on. Washington too, was informed by Pilsudski that he was ready to move, if the Germans were to disturb the international order. Nonetheless, reaction in the West remained negative, almost into 1939.

In the East, though, something was afoot. While handwritten notes were moved across the table during sessions of the Central Committee, discussing the best time for the planned attack on Europe, the USSR acted quite differently on the international stage. Convinced of the superiority of its own clandestine rearmament, the USSR, during those years, swamped international conferences with proposals to disarm. Furthermore, a whole system of non-aggression pacts were proposed for Eastern

Europe. Finally, in 1932, a Russian-Polish nonaggression pact was concluded. Full of distrust, an attack was defined in such a way that any "intrusion" or "attack by means of land, sea or air forces, even if not accompanied by a declaration of war" should be considered an aggression, while specifying "no considerations of a political, military, economic or other nature, could be used … as reasons for excuse or justification".

Also excluded as reasons for an attack were "the internal situation" of a state "e.g. its political, economic or social order" and "alleged deficiencies in it administration". From that time on, Warsaw assumed to have neutralized the USSR. Nothing changed up to the outbreak of the war. A joint declaration, issued on 26 November 1938, confirmed the continued existence of the non-aggression pact, even under the conditions changed by the Munich Agreement.[31] Thus, from 1932 onward, the Soviet Union no longer had any legal justification for an attack on Poland. On the other hand, in 1932 and 1933, a Polish attack in the West was more imminent than some people realized. This is shown by two letters written by the future Polish foreign minister Beck, to Pilsudski.

---

[31] For the text, see DVPS, XXI, doc. 468, p. 650, cf. Bartel, Frankreich, S. 89. cf. also Polish White Book, doc. 160, p. 234.

"Once the leaders of the republic's foreign policy have succeeded in guaranteeing the security of the Eastern borders of the state by the conclusion of a non-aggression pact with Soviet Russia, there is only one significant aspect: it has freed our hands with respect to Germany." [32]

With these words, Colonel Joseph Beck, in October 1932, while still assistant minister of foreign affairs, appealed to Marshal Pilsudski, the dictatorial leader of the state. He demanded the immediate attack against Germany and referred to the non-aggression pact with the USSR about to be concluded. The conditions for a "war to liberate Polish territories from the German yoke" were therefore as favorable as never before. The army was ready.

In Germany, the authorities in 1932 were under no illusions as to an impending Polish attack. Reichswehr minister Gröner travelled to East Prussia as early as March of that year, and, in a number of articles and speeches, warned Poland not to attack. From that time on, authorities in East Prussia began with the construction of an improvised line of defenses, in an effort at least to slow down a Polish march on Königsberg, if

---

[32] Report, p. 3, dated 4 November 1932, of the Federal Police Directorate in Vienna addressed to the Austrian Federal Chancellor Dollfuss concerning a letter written by Beck to Pilsudski on 27 October 1932; the report includes a partial copy of said letter, reproduction owned by the author, here p. 1.

it should come to that. Upon receipt of Beck's letter, Pilsudski increased his foreign policy efforts. He valued the colonel's opinions; the two men had, after all, fought together in the Polish Legion in the First World War. Later on, Pilsudski chose Beck for the diplomatic service.

Only a few days after receiving the letter he promoted him from assistant minister to the head of the Polish foreign policy. In the end, he formally assigned him to this post thus ensuring that, up to the catastrophe of 1939 when he felt the conditions for a war against Germany to be fulfilled, Beck was largely able to act as he pleased as long as he could claim to be backed by the Marshal.

In the winter of 1932, Beck wanted to become the foreign minister of the attack on Germany. For this end, he acted quickly and decidedly. Over the preceding months, there had been lengthy debates with France, due to the fact that the French government while doing little for its eastern ally, was always ready to raise all sorts of objections to underline its central role. At the time, there were disputes concerning non-aggression pact with the USSR, signed but not yet ratified, which Paris would only accept if such an agreement were also concluded with Romania, but Bucharest was not particularly eager to follow suit. Beck did away with this conflict.

The French government "wants to restrain us" and is thinking of a settlement with Germany, he wrote to Pilsudski. In any case, Germany's weakness was a temporary phenomenon, he said, which would have to be exploited now or never. "If that is not taken into account, neither we nor our children will live to see a Greater Poland".[33] The Russian-Polish non-aggression pact was ratified on 27 November 1932.

The road into Germany was now open, provided the Western powers reacted as intended and did not consider Poland's new self-assertion to be just another foray of a powerless grumbler rather than a valuable ally. Warsaw's idea was that such an ally would have to wooed by promising him, if necessary, another piece of German territory. In an effort to show Paris that "we can use other means", Pilsudski was soon to kick out the French military mission in a highly offensive manner and to be "absent" for French diplomats. This was in line with Beck's new maxim:

"An independent Polish policy is possible and required. France is obligated to take Polish interests into account just as much

---

[33] Report of the Federal Police Directorate in Vienna, addressed to the Austrian Federal Chancellor Dollfuss concerning a letter written by Beck to Pilsudski, here p. 3.

as we must take French interests into account".[34]

At the same time, Beck, in line with what he had sketched out for Pilsudski, chose a confrontational course with respect to a particularly sensitive and well-known issue: "The Polish-German conflict must be given a sharper outline. A year earlier, Beck had considered an occupation of Danzig to be "possibly necessary at a later date", but not at the moment.[35] Still, over the months that followed, he aggravated the situation at Danzig, for example by insisting – contrary to valid legal dispositions – on the entry into the Danzig port of the Polish destroyer Wicher.

The ship had previously been instructed to open fire on "the nearest public building" in case of an "insult" by the Danzig senate.[36] March 1933 saw increasing troop concentrations in the area between Danzig and Thorn destined to be used for a simultaneous attack on Danzig, East Prussia and East Pomerania, in accordance with a scenario elaborated jointly with the French in 1923.[37]

For the moment, these moves remained ineffective. The Western powers held back, and

---

[34] Beck to Pilsudski, 30 October 1932, p. 2.
[35] Cf. Denne, Danzig-Problem, p. 28.
[36] Cf. Denne, Danzig-Problem, p. 29.
[37] Cf. Roos, Polen, p. 6.

in Germany, the national-socialist Government to be appointed a few weeks later, did not react to the Polish provocations. On the contrary, it showed itself to be prepared to accept Polish demands which, earlier on, had been rejected by the Weimar government. Such a situation Beck, in his letter to Pilsudski had regarded as impossible. Later, Beck would complain that "we were forced to conclude agreements with these completely unrestrained neighbors".[38] "By tomorrow, it will be to late to strip Germany of the ancestral Polish lands which, today, one could return to the republic" he had written in 1932.[39] This kind of assessment would be put on the back burner in the years to come.

There may never have been a conflict of such dimensions, whose momentum would be overlooked so completely both in the Western capitals at the time and in present-day historiography; whatever texts we have, begin with the year 1939 and totally fail to deal with the antecedents of the German-Polish war. This is, however, not surprising as the Oder-Neisse line was actually adopted after 1945; in a similar way, it is not surprising that NS-policies were cited as an official pretext for these actions.

---

[38] Quoted from Wehner, Polen-Politik, p. 146.
[39] Beck to Pilsudski, 27 October 1932, p. 3.

As early as the summer of 1938, the League of Nations High Commissioner for Danzig, Carl Jacob Burckhardt saw through the policy of the Polish foreign minister and clearly recognized its consequences:

"The Poles are waiting, seemingly at ease. While we were travelling through the night, Beck let me in a little on his plans. He was going on with his double game. It is not a German game as many Frenchmen and the Polish opposition like to think. It is a game were Poland gambles for the highest stakes, a jackpot that is to result from a final and unavoidable catastrophe for Germany ... Warsaw is not only silently hoping for an unconditional integration of Danzig, but for a lot more, for all of East Prussia, for Silesia, even Pomerania thrown in for good measure. In 1933, there was still talk of Polish Pomerelia, but now it's "our Pomerania". Since the reoccupation of the Rhineland and French immobility on that occasion, Beck has been carrying out a purely Polish policy, anti-German in the end, only pretended to be aiming for Polish-German détente. But they are methodically trying to encourage the Germans in their mistakes".[40]

According to Burckhardt, Beck has successfully contributed his share to establishing the NS-regime as the enemy by the

---

[40] Quoted from Burckhardt, Mission, p. 156 et seq.

summer of 1938. In any case, he was able to undertake at that time first steps towards an alliance with the West. British policy finally went on the move. In this vein, Duff Cooper, at the time First Lord of the Admiralty and one of the most pronounced advocates of an anti-German British policy, went on a tour of the Baltic. On 8 August, he met Beck at Gdynia. This became one of those strange meetings which were later shrouded in silence, although there are no doubts as to its fundamental importance.

At that time and during those discussions, a British-Polish alliance began to take shape. After the war, the Polish ambassador at London, Edward Raczynski would testify to this and none other than the British Foreign Secretary at the time, Halifax, agreed with him in the foreword to the book. Beck had been planning for years to move the Allies to back up the Polish cause. Now he was able to say that he could "within 24 hours join the Allies".[41] Understandably, he wanted something in return from the Western powers, in the form of land and rights. Not being certain, however, that London and Paris would actually become militarily active against Germany, Beck also wanted to profit from another German bounty. Hence, in peace with Hitler, in war against him, so Beck defined his policy at two meetings in

---

[41] Cf. Roos, Polen, p. 347.

the Warsaw palace.[42] Autumn of 1938, after all, brought another "peace" in the form of the Munich Agreement which approved a carving up of Czechoslovakia. As he had said, Beck, in this case, went "with Hitler" and ensured a part of the country for Poland.

---

[42] Cf. Beck, Report, p. 162, also Roos, Polen, p. 331.

Execution – Western offensive guarantee and Eastern backing

„Whatever they all say, everybody, openly or secretly, is hoping the Poles will come down again. But the whole House expects war."

Henry Channon (Diary entry regarding the mood in the British *Parliament, 24 August 1939)[43]*

German-Polish cooperation at the expense of Czechoslovakia did not in any way change Poland's basic position or the guidance of its foreign policy. When, in October 1938, the Berlin government attempted to win over Poland as a partner by offering a long-term agreement including the recognition of the existing Polish border with Germany – heretofore refused by all German governments since 1919 – Warsaw refused. Berlin had not asked Warsaw for a joint action against the USSR as has often been claimed. At first, Beck drew out the negotiations without really saying no. In late 1938 and early 1939, he at last received messages indicating a possible decision on the part of the Western powers.

---

[43] Sir Henry Channon (1897-1958), MP since 1935. Diary entry made after the session of the British Parliament the same day. Quoted here from Gilbert, Documents, p. 1596.

The Polish ambassador at Washington, Jerzy Potocki, had for a year been hinting at an increased U.S. readiness to go to war against Germany. By the end of 1938, his reports had become so antisemitic that they could by taken to be products of German propaganda – in the end, after the occupation of Warsaw, they were effectively used in this manner. Potocki confirmed repeatedly German prejudices against the way in which foreign policy decisions were arrived at in Washington and the influence which Jewish groups and personalities in these matters:

"The American public is exposed to a permanent alarmist propaganda which is under Jewish influence and incessantly conjures the specter of a war; compared to last year, the Americans have thus strongly changed their attitude towards problems of foreign policy".[44]

More or less, Potocki stated that the American public was in Jewish hands, and attempted, in this report, to prove his point by means of polls. Three days later, he derided the ongoing campaign against Germany and the "totalitarian states" because the Soviet Union was completely excluded from this campaign and was presented to the public as belonging to the

---

[44] Report by Potocki to the Polish minister of foreign affairs, dated 9 January 1939, quoted from AA, Roosevelts Weg, S. 59 et seq.

democratic camp.[45] A psychosis of war was being intentionally fomented. Potocki correctly and clearly separated cause and effect, however saying that it was German policy which became increasingly more and more radical:

> *"Furthermore, it is the German actions against the Jews and the problem of the immigrants, which continue to stir up the hatred of anything connected to National Socialism. Individual Jewish intellectuals have taken part in this movement, e.g. Bernard Baruch, or the governor of the state of New York, Lehmann, the newly appointed judge of the Supreme Court, Felix Frankfurter, Treasury Secretary Morgenthau and others who are personal friends of president Roosevelt. They want the president to become an active promoter of human rights, of religious freedom and freedom of expression and want him to start punishing troublemakers."[46]*

These reports – the existence of which became known in Berlin in January 1939 – had a considerable effect on the outbreak of the war in late summer of that year. Poland could base her decisions on the enmity of the USA against

---

[45] Report by Potocki to the Polish minister of foreign affairs, dated 12 January 1939, quoted from AA, Roosevelts Weg, p. 63 et seq.
[46] Report by Potocki to the Polish minister of foreign affairs, dated 12 January 1939, quoted from AA, Roosevelts Weg, p. 64.

the present German regime. Reports from London and Paris found in Warsaw confirm that in those countries as well, the US ambassadors, ordered to do so by the president, acted massively in favor of a war against Germany and were increasingly effective in this. In London this was supported by Winston Churchill and his companions and by the Admiralty – they "favored war at any price", in the words of the former German chancellor Brüning in exile in Britain.[47]

Thus, the ground had been prepared for a development which Warsaw had envisioned for years. If the "West" moved against Germany, Poland had to be part of it. Accordingly, when the German foreign minister came to Warsaw with new proposals on 24 January, he was diplomatically snubbed. "Because of an illness", Josef Beck called off a dinner speech that had already been prepared and began to arrange his trip to London in February. One of the items on the agenda were the rewards for Poland's war plans against Germany. The official British documents contain Beck's message to stating that Beck wanted to talk about "colonies, Jews, and Danzig".[48]

---

[47] Note by Brüning about 'Eindrücke in England', March 1939, quoted from Brüning, Briefe, I, p. 233.
[48] Cf. DBFP, III. Series, Vol. IV, doc. 175, p. 181, 4 March 1939, telegram Kennard to Halifax.

He thus announced the anti-Jewish feelings of most of the Polish parties, in addition to those of his government which "openly embraced Antisemitism", including, last not least, foreign minister Beck himself.[49] This was very much in the tradition of the countrywide anti-Jewish boycott of 1912; the ultimate goal was the emigration of most, if not all Jews from Poland. Furthermore, Poland eyed a large piece of the former German colonial possessions in Africa and, of course, sovereignty over Danzig.

There may well have been more that was discussed in London at the time. In his London exile, Heinrich Brüning was informed of a British-Polish agreement on partition (of Germany) which he mentioned in several private letters and to which he attributed a great share of the responsibility for the outbreak of the war: "Do you think that any one of us, after the summer of 1940, would have been able to change in any way the fact that Poland risked a war on account of the promise by the British government that she would receive not only East Prussia but Upper Silesia as well?"[50]

---

[49] E.g. Nachum Goldmann, president of the World Jewish Congress, after a conversation with Beck. Cf. Goldmann, Paradox, p. 206 et seq.

[50] HUG FP 93.10, Box 4, File: Arnold, Clara Brecht. Brüning to A. Brecht, 2 September 1946, p. 1, quoted here from Volkmann, Brüning, p. 339.

Both objectives had been announced to the Western powers by Polish agencies as early as 1919. It is obvious that this had now been reiterated and agreed on, while Brüning, as a potential representative of a new democratic German Government, had been informed that this was the price to pay for a peace agreement. He declared that he would not sign anything like that. Actually, Polish requests went far beyond this, as was expressed by the president of the Polish national-democratic party, Kowalski, who had demanded the Oder-Neisse line in a speech in April 1939 and had thought it to be a good idea to put this down on paper.[51]

During the war, the Polish underground government printed a map in the form of a postage stamp, labeled "This is what we are fighting for". It showed the Polish state stretching from the Baltic down to the Black Sea, including Germany east of the Oder and Neisse rivers, Slovakia, Lithuania, White Russia, the western Ukraine, but also the former German colonies Cameroon and East Africa.[52] In addition, the French island of Madagascar was shown to be Polish; since the mid-1930s, it had been eyed by Beck's government as a "Devil's island for the Jews" (Shlomo Aronson). The phrase "colonies, Jews, and Danzig" was not used haphazardly.

---

[51] Cf. Kowalski, Polska, passim.
[52] Printed as a facsimile in Scheil, Churchill, p. 181.

Josef Beck was very pleased when he went back home. He could now decide whether a war would take place or not. Britain had pledged her help if Poland had to take up arms because of a "direct or indirect" threat. An attack by a foreign country was not needed for the guarantee to be activated; moreover, a further amendment extended the casus foederis to conflicts between third countries if "this is an obvious threat to the security of one of the contracting parties". Such a situation could thus occur if Poland felt threatened and went to war. For the first time in British history, a decision of this magnitude had been placed into the hands of a foreign power, as Alexander Cadogan, permanent Undersecretary of the British Foreign Office declared somewhat emotionally.[53]

The metaphor of a British "blank cheque", occasionally used in this connection, describes the situation correctly, from a formal viewpoint. Poland had become the master of a British war against Germany which "any gesture of Germany" could unleash. Precisely this clause was invoked by the Warsaw government for Danzig on 10 August 1939 after the German foreign office had expressed its "astonishment" on the subject of a previous Polish ultimatum addressed to the Danzig municipality:

---

[53] Quoted from FRUS 1939, I, p. 105 et seq.

"The Polish government will ... regard any future interference of the German government, prejudicial to the rights and interests [at Danzig, author], as an act of war."[54]

Any future German letter concerning Danzig could thus be construed, in an extreme case, to be an act of war calling for the British guarantee. In the same way, the conditions of the French Polish military agreement would be fulfilled; precisely this Danzig scenario had been described there in May 1939 as a case in point. A major French attack would take place as guaranteed and decide the war against Germany on the battlefield. Danzig scenario had been described there in May 1939 as a case in point. A major French attack would take place as guaranteed and decide the war against Germany on the battlefield.

In the East, the Soviet Union did everything in its power to reassure the Polish republic. In November 1938, both sides had, in a joint declaration reiterated the validity of the 1932 non-aggression pact. To underline this, the assistant Soviet foreign minister, Potemkin travelled to Warsaw. He declared that in the case of a German attack, Poland had nothing to fear from the Soviet Union. On the contrary, Poland could count on Soviet friendship and on the supply of ammunition and other war

---

[54] Polish White Book, doc. 86, 10 August 1939, p. 129.

material. Josef Beck and the Pilsudskites in Warsaw government circles had every right to feel that their situation was safe and secure.

Poland began immediately to prepare the conflict with Germany. On a military level, this entailed the mobilization of the army which, as early as March, comprised several hundred thousand men. Nothing comparable took place on the German side.[55] Within Poland, measures against the ethnic German population were reinforced. Camps intended to take in the Germans were set up in March. Violence against Germans, German firms and German property increased and caused a wave of some 70 000 refugees to flee to Germany. Throughout the summer, the number of violent incidents along the Polish-German border increased. [56]

The population registered this with satisfaction. A Polish customs officer expressed his worry to the departing Germans; they should not go over to the other side, as Germany had already lost the war. When the German military police took note of this on 26 August 1939, it did not even

---

[55] This factual statement would cause political turmoil in Germany many years later when it was mentioned by Erika Steinbach, president of the German Association of Expellees, before the CDU fraction of the German federal parliament.

[56] Cf. BA-MA RH 24-14/80 Bl. 12, Bericht Geheime Feldpolizei dated 28 August 1939.

mention this as anything special. Throughout the Polish-German borderlands, such reports abounded in the latter half of the month. They included rumors about German war plans and about potential Polish strikes against certain German radio stations, but also about Polish posters in the border area explaining why the war against Germany had to be carried out now, and why the chances were good.[57]

The public was roused with reports of offensives against the city of Berlin and with a new border along the Oder river.[58] A German mole in the Polish general staff even spoke of an attack on Germany without a declaration of war.[59] This report reached the German airforce stationed close to the border on 24 August. The future warring nations mobilized in every possible manner, both militarily and propagandistically. It was a war of nerves before the real war and Warsaw, in late August, believed that Germany had already lost it.[60]

Finally, on 1st September 1939, Hitler, the leader of the German state, of the government and of the party, stepped out and told the world,

---

[57] Cf. BA-MA RH 24-14/80, Bl. 17.
[58] Cf. BA-MA RL 3/1822, report of 27 June 1939, Bl. 5.
[59] Cf. RL 7/330, Kriegstagebuch des Luftflottenkommandos 4.
[60] Cf. RL 7/330, Bl. 10, announcement of Polish radio.

that "fire had been returned" for several hours.[61] He was referring to the German attack on Poland which had just begun and he considered it to be not only a reaction to Polish warmongering sponsored by Britain, but also a direct response to alleged Polish armed intrusions into German territory, as he underlined.

Over the months that followed, all the warring parties would undertake a slugging match by means of government publications, discussing the truth of all this. There was a French "Yellow Book", a British "Blue Book" and a Polish "White Book" which Germany countered with her own publications. The German foreign office compiled nearly 500 documents, including a list of 44 places and dates where Poland allegedly had caused border incidents.[62] The most famous of them would become the attack on the (German) Gleiwitz radio station which a witness at Nuremberg described as having been organized by an SS commando. For all practical purposes, it was disregarded by the German propaganda throughout the war.[63]

---

[61] Cf. Hitler's speech before the Reichstag on 1st September, in: AA, Vorgeschichte, p. 448.

[62] Locations of border crossings by regular Polish troops were mentioned as Neukrug (twice), Scharschau, Pfalzdorf und Röhrsdorf. Cf.. AA, Vorgeschichte, p.. 443.
et seq.

[63] In this case, see the more extensive presentation in my book "Fünf plus Zwei", chapter "Von Paris nach

The foreign office, too, had never maintained that regular Polish troops had operated there. After 1945, the collective memory somehow became focused on this incident, totally oblivious of the fact that the summer of 1939 had been a highly complicated and critical time of mutual threats and mobilizations.

In fact, towards the end of August of that year, shooting incidents were daily occurrences along the German-Polish border – originating on either side. Numerous documents in the German federal archive – which, at the time, were not prepared or published for political purposes bear this out. A German army instruction allowed to fire in case of Polish border trespasses with obvious aggressive intent.[64] Another order stated that Polish incursions by regular or irregular forces should not be allowed to grow into major battles. Both sides were interested in putting the blame for a real war on the other side. Hence, Poland's military commander, Edward Rydz-Smigly refused to follow the suggestions of his general

---

Gleiwitz". Teile einsehbar im Netz: http://www.symposion.org/Gleiwitz.htm
[64] Cf. BA-MA RH 24-8/13, order of VIII. AK dated 21 August 1939, 18:30 h.

to attack the German forces in Silesia – he feared negative reactions abroad.[65]

Gleiwitz as well had become an object of military speculation even before the war broke out. The symbolic significance of the city became apparent shortly before and after 1st September. A German undercover agent in Poland, on 27 August, reported that the city could not be defended by the Germans.[66] A report by the German customs office at Gleiwitz stated on 1st September that the Polish school in neighboring Hindenburg (Germany) had been occupied by armed Poles who could not be driven out of the building and who were shooting into the surrounding area.[67] Moreover, in the vicinity, Polish army units had repulsed a foray by German irregulars into Polish territory.

A messenger from Myslowitz reported that the Polish "occupation of Gleiwitz" was widely welcomed on the Polish side.[68] People in the area were waiting for further actins along these lines. Reports of the Polish army were similar. On 6 September 1939, it was reported that Polish officers were informing their units about

---

[65] Cf. The presentation of the Polish general Rómmel in: Za honor I ojczyne (For honor and fatherland), Warsaw 1958, Rundschau, 9/1959, p. 496.
[66] Cf. BA-MA RH 24-10/244, Bl. 83, situation Poland N°. 12 of 27 August 1939.
[67] Cf. BA-MA RH 24-14/80, Bl. 92.
[68] Cf. BA-MA RH 24-14/80b, Bl. 109, report of 2 September 1939, Source: Refugee from Myslowitz.

the 'progress of the Polish army on Berlin'. The soldiers learned that Polish troops had already conquered Danzig, half of East Prussia, and Gleiwitz. When the soldiers objected that they were constantly on retreat, the officers simply explained that the Germans had identified the weakest section of the Polish front.[69]

Along these lines, readily available information mixed with popular disinformation and shaped an overall picture which at least was correct in one sense: As the Polish customs officer had said, Germany had already lost the war, not the military war against Poland, but the war of nerves and the upcoming world war.[70] For the Polish-German conflict, contrary to what Warsaw and Berlin had been planning, did turn into a world war. Hitler's government had allowed itself to be carried away into a military strike for which it had initially been careful to avoid the word "war" in an effort to be able to limit the operations. On 2 September, London was explicitly informed that the German troops

---

[69] BA-MA RH 24-14/80b, Bl. 140, report of 6 September 1939, source: V-90.

[70] Concerning this assessment: "Various sources in Poland report again and again on the Polish view concerning success in a future war, in the sense that Poland believes 'Germany will have tactical gains initially, but they will not attain the strategic goal in the long run, just as they were unable to attain it in the World War because of a lack of raw materials.'. Quoted after BA-MA RL 3/1822, report of 27 June 1939, Bl. 5.

would be withdrawn in the case of concessions and a termination of Polish provocations.

Poland, on the other hand, maintained her policy up to the very end. As late as 31 August, the Polish ambassador to Berlin declared "that he had no reason to be interested in German notes or German propositions. After all, he knew the situation in Germany very well, having spent five and a half years in the country as ambassador, and had close relations with Göring and other influential circles. He declared to be convinced that, in the case of a war, turmoil would erupt in the country and that Polish troops would successfully advance towards Berlin".[71]

The background of this statement included the "16 points", German proposals that had been presented to ambassador Lipski that very morning by a British diplomat and the Swedish go-between Dahlerus. They contained i.a. a proposal for plebiscites on controversial questions and underlined the German readiness to accept the Polish borders, as they stood at the time, in the case of a German defeat in a plebiscite. They were too moderate to be presented to the international public, hence it was better to ignore them completely.

---

[71] Cf. Dahlerus, Versuch, p. 110.

In London, Winston Churchill's war party personally made sure that British papers would not report on the issue. Poland, based on the erroneous assumptions about the internal weakness of the NS-regime as they had been spread by the German opposition, was ready to risk a military match. Even two years later, the German head of state still mused about Lipski's ideas:

"Overall, there was this assumption that Germany would immediately crumble. In one of his report, Lipski writes that he knew from an official source that Germany would crumble within a week."[72]

It was only logical that a telegram from Warsaw, addressed to Lipski one day before the outbreak of hostilities, which the Germans decoded, stated unmistakably:

"Do not enter into any kind of factual discussions; if the Reich government makes any proposals in writing, you must declare that you have no authority to receive or discuss such proposals and that your only task is to transmit the above-mentioned note from your government while waiting for further instructions".[73]

That was only logical. After all, Beck had sought and found guarantors for a Polish policy

---

[72] Hitler in one of his "Tischgespräche", quoted after Jochmann, Monologe, p. 253, entry of 2 January 1942.
[73] Cf. Dahlerus, Versuch, p. 113.

which aimed for an offensive solution of the allegedly unavoidable German-Polish conflict, covered in the East by the Polish non-aggression pact with the Soviet Union and supported in the West by the offensive alliance with Britain and France. No one in Warsaw would entertain the idea of letting this singularly promising situation worked for by Beck since late 1932 be spoiled by negotiations or by allowing hesitant sections of British diplomacy to bale out. The Polish representative in London, Raczynski, was working in close cooperation with Winston Churchill's war party in a joint effort to crush any remaining opposition in the government. Thus, at the end of August 1939, all trumps in this game of foreign policy were seemingly held by Beck and the efforts of several years had apparently borne fruit. Beck had

- neutralized the Soviet Union and thus protected Poland's back. The USSR had not only promised a benevolent neutrality but also the supply of arms.

- concluded an unconditional alliance with the Western powers France and Britain, applicable in any kind of war scenario. Moreover, taken together they were not only economically and militarily stronger than Germany, they also controlled, directly or indirectly, some forty percent of the

Earth's surface and could thus fulfill any Polish wishes with respect to colonies.

- assured himself of the good will the United States and its active support of the ongoing policy of the three European partners. Bullitt, Ambassador to Paris and one of the major figures of US diplomacy, had even promised an American entry into the war.

- Received clear signals from Germany indicating that the National Socialist state was suffering from basic differences and a pessimistic view of any war into the highest diplomatic and military circles and would not survive a major crisis.

As the Polish ambassador to Berlin, Lipski, had announced to the British diplomat Forbes on the morning of 31 August 1939, the following scenario should now take place: a military conflict, internal unrest in Germany and a march of Polish troops on Berlin. This would be supported by British air raids and a massive French offensive in the West, promised to occur within two weeks. Poland would, at least, gain Danzig and parts of East Prussia plus those colonies which Beck had claimed in the negotiations six months earlier and which were crucial for the peace negotiations after a victory, as the Polish ministry of foreign affairs noted a few days into the war.[74]

This optimistic schedule of events was to receive, after 1st September, a first blow by the unexpected stability of the NS-regime. Numerous sources, from the general staff to the conservative opposition, had promised the Allies an overthrow of the German government. It did not take place. A joint French and British all-out offensive, promised in the agreements, would have ended the war by a German defeat. Hardly any German forces were available to oppose such an action in the West. The units fighting against Poland in the East were worn out.

Even the ammunition available for the fight against Poland had been used up and the German advance had to be halted on certain occasions. A defense against a French attack would have broken down immediately for similar reasons. However, both the Western powers and the Soviet Union reneged on their obligations. This was not immediately apparent and well into the second week of the war, Warsaw was optimistic. Poland urged the Western powers to take action which would still have been possible within the time frame laid out in the agreements. The Polish army was told that, even if a particular force was in retreat,

---

[74] Cf. Lubienski, Polen, p. 80.

others were on their way to Berlin and the others would eventually follow. It was said that the major French offensive had already started. The Soviet Union, too, kept its neutrality as expected.

Then everything fell to pieces. The Allied War Council, on 12 September, decided officially what the French and British military authorities had mapped out in the spring. In spite of all oral promises and the legally binding signatures on official letterheads, Poland would, in the end, receive no support. It was thought to be better to draw out the war with Germany for something like three years, what would then be done with the defeated Polish state remained to be seen. At that moment, and probably for that reason, the Soviet Union, on 17 September, broke the Polish-Soviet non-aggression pact and attacked Poland, international law notwithstanding.

It is difficult to find parallels in history for such behavior. Josef Beck's policy, the policy of the colonels from Pilsudski's Polish legion – regardless of what they had done or not done – fell victim to one of the most blatant political deceptions in recorded history.

Summary – Questions and answers

Did Poland raise demands for German territory since the end of the 19th century onwards? – Yes.

Were these demands limited to areas with an ethnic Polish majority? No.

Were these demands limited to areas which had been inhabited, at one time or another in history, by an ethnic Polish majority? No.

Were these demands limited to regions that had belonged to the Polish state at the moment of its partitions in 1772? No.

Were academic institution set up in Poland in 1919 whose task it was to justify further demands? Yes.

Did the Polish government or Polish political parties aim for plebiscites in the areas they demanded? No.

Were Polish political parties ever able to gain even a single seat in the Reichstag within the later German borders? No.

Was the Polish side able to win a single one of the plebiscites held under Allied supervision in the disputed regions? No.

Did the Polish government accept the results of the plebiscites held in Silesia and East Prussia which, in certain areas, gave Germany a majority of 97.5 percent of the votes cast? No.

Did Polish terrorists attempt on several occasions to disrupt the plebiscite in Silesia by force? Yes.

Did Polish parties and politicians accept the ethnic structures as they existed around 1900? No.

Was a systematic policy of expulsion carried out after 1919 against ethnic Germans who lived in areas that had become Polish on account of the new borders? Yes.

Was this policy of expulsion implemented by a long-range program of expropriation concerning real estate owned by Germans? Yes.

Was the closure of German schools part of this policy of expulsion? Yes.

Was the dismissal of German workers and employees part of this policy of expulsion? Yes.

Did Polish politicians including the head of the government explicitly negate the right to exist of the German ethnic minority in Poland? Yes.

Did the Polish republic approach London and Paris on several occasions for help with an attack on Germany? Yes.

Did the Polish threats of war become so serious around 1930 as to cause Germany to undertake large-scale defensive measures and draw up evacuation plans for whole areas? Yes.

Did members of the Polish general staff at that time demand the removal of the German capital from Berlin to Frankfurt on Main on the grounds that Berlin was on Slavic soil? Yes.

Did the Polish government, in early winter 1932, attempt to provoke a conflict in Danzig? Yes.

Did the Polish government, in 1936, assure the Western powers that, in spite of the non-aggression pact then in force, it continued to stand ready for an attack on Germany? Yes.

Did the Warsaw foreign ministry, in the summer of 1938, plan to join the Western powers in a possible war against Germany? Yes.

Did the Polish government, in 1939, hide the German proposals for negotiations about Danzig and the German-Polish border from France and Britain? Yes.

Did Poland, in early 1939, prepare concentration camps for the local Germans? Yes.

Did Poland, in early 1939, prepare lists of names of Germans who were to be marched into these concentration camps? Yes.

Were more than 5000 Germans killed during these marches and the ensuing violence? Yes.

Did Polish politicians, in the spring of 1939, call for the conquest of German lands up to the Oder-Neisse line? Yes.

Did Polish politicians draw up plans for borders to the west of the Oder river and for the partitioning of the eastern parts of today's Germany? Yes.

Are the statements of senior Western diplomats correct that such plans were entertained in the Polish ministry of foreign affairs and by the foreign minister himself? Yes.

Were ethnic cleansings of local Germans carried out in late 1938 in the Czechoslovak areas recently conquered by Poland? Yes.

Did a former German chancellor and opponent of the NS-regime state to have seen a British-Polish agreement which, in early 1939, promised parts of Eastern Germany to Poland in the case of a war? Yes.

Was Poland first to mobilize her army in 1939? Yes.

Did Polish officers, including the army chief of staff, plan for a war in the spring of 1939 and did they declare that such a war would be carried out offensively? Yes.

Did the Polish government, on 5 August 1939, utter a threat of war against Germany because of a letter it had received from the German government on the subject of Danzig? Yes.

Did the Polish government, in late August 1939, expressly refuse to accept any kind of proposals for negotiations from the German side? Yes.

Did excesses against local Germans take place in Poland before 1st September 1939, causing the flight of some 70 000 Germans to Germany? Yes.

Did Polish troops shoot at German installations and airplanes before 1before 1st September 1939? Yes.

Did Polish troops and irregulars violate the German border before 1st September 1939? Yes.

Did this also occur near the well-known city of Gleiwitz? Yes.

Were Polish soldiers told that the objective of the coming war was a march on Berlin? Yes.

Did the Polish ambassador to Berlin, in the morning of 31st August 1939 declare that Polish troops would soon march on Berlin? Yes.

Did members of the Polish government in exile, demand once again parts of eastern Germany after the autumn of 1939? Yes.

Did they, on those occasions, again demand the expulsion of the local German population? Yes.

Did the Polish politicians, at that point in time, entertain any illusions causing them to doubt the German character of the lands in question? No.

Literature

Baginski, Henryk: Poland's Freedom of the Sea, Kirkcaldy 1942 (zit. "Freedom")

- Poland and the Baltic, London 1942 (zit. "Poland")

Bierschenk, Theodor: Die Deutsche Volksgruppe in Polen, 1934–1939, Kitzingen 1954 (zit. "Volksgruppe")

Blanke, Richard: Orphans of Versailles - The Germans in Western Poland 1918-1939, Lexongton 1993 ("Versailles")

Brier, Robert: Der polnische "Westgedanke" nach dem Zweiten Weltkrieg, (Magisterarbeit) Digitale Osteuropa-Bibliothek 2003 (zit. "Westgedanke")

Burckhardt, Carl J.: Meine Danziger Mission, München 1960 (zit. "Mission")

Conze, Werner: Polnische Nation und deutsche Politik im Ersten Weltkrieg, Köln 1958 (zit. "Nation")

Gehrke, Roland: Der polnische Westgedanke bis zur Wiedererrichtung des polnischen Staates nach Ende des Ersten Weltkriegs, Marburg 2001 (zit. "Westgedanke")

Gelberg, Ludwik: Die Entstehung der Volksrepublik Polen, Die völkerrechtlichen Probleme, Frankfurt 1972 (zit. "Entstehung")

Giertych, Jedrzej: Die Frage der Wiedergewonnenen Gebiete im Lichte der Ethik,

Stuttgart 1949 (dt. Übersetzung des poln. Originals von 1948 für den Dienstgebrauch, zit. "Gebiete")

- Poł wieku polskiej polityki, London 1947

Kisielewski, Jozef: Ziemia gromadzi prochy, Posen o.J (ca. 1938/39) - (Die Erde bewahrt das Vergangene) Poznan 1939 (Berlin, dienstl. Übersetzung 1939) (zit. "Erde")

Kornat, Marek: Polen zwischen Hitler und Stalin - Studien zur polnischen Außenpolitik in der Zwischenkriegszeit, Berlin 2012 (zit. "Polen")

Kowalski, Kazimierz: Polska wobec Niemiec, Przemówienie Kazimierza Kowalskiego, prezesa Zarządu Głównego Stronnictwa Narodowego, wygłoszone na zjeździe działaczy politycznych SN w diu 30.4.1939 r. w Warszawie, Warszawa 1939 (Poland and Germany. Speech of Kazimierz Kowalski, Chairman of the National Party, at the meeting of the political funktionaries of the Party in Warsaw, 30. April1939) (zit. "Polska")

Krzoska, Markus: Für ein Polen an Oder und Ostsee - Zygmunt Wojciechowski (1900-1955) als Historiker und Publizist, Osnabrück 2003 (zit. "Wojciechowski")

Laeuen, Harald: Polnisches Zwischenspiel, Berlin 1940

Lutoslawski, Wincenty: The Polish Nation - A Lecture delivered at the Lowell Institute in Boston on October 21, 1907, and at the University of California on March 9, 1908

- Gdańsk and East Prussia (Polish Commission of work preparatory to the Conference of Peace), Paris 1919 (auch Neudruck Nendeln 1973) (zit. "Gdańsk")

Marx, Karl: Herr Vogt, Moskau 1941 (1860)

Neumann, Josef (Hrsg.): Beiträge zur Lösung der polnischen Frage, Berlin 1916

Oertzen, Friedrich Wilhelm: Das ist Polen, München 1932

Porter, Brian: When Nationalism began to hate - Imagining Modern Politics in Nineteenth–Century Poland, Oxford 2000

Prazmowska, Anita: Britain, Poland and the Eastern Front, 1939, (Soviet and East European Studies), Cambridge 1987

- Britain and Poland 1939–1943, The betrayed ally, Cambridge 1995

Roos, Hans (=Hans-Otto Meissner): Polen und Europa, Studien zur polnischen Außenpolitik 1931–1939, Tübingen 1957 (zit. "Polen")

Roth, Paul: Die politische Entwicklung in Kongreßpolen während der deutschen Okkupation, Leipzig 1919 (zit. "Kongreßpolen")

Scheil, Stefan: Logik der Mächte, Europas Problem mit der Globalisierung der Politik, Überlegungen zur Vorgeschichte des Zweiten Weltkrieges, Berlin 1999 (zit. "Logik")

- Churchill, Hitler, und der Antisemitismus, Berlin 2009 (zit. „Churchill")
- Fünf plus Zwei, Die europäischen Nationalstaaten, die Weltmächte und die vereinte Entfesselung des Zweiten Weltkriegs, Berlin 2003 (zit. "Vereinte Entfesselung")

Terry, Sarah Meiklejohn: Polands Place in Europe, General Sikorski and the Origin of the Oder–Neisse–Line 1939–1943, Princeton 1983 (zit. "Place")

List of Abbreviations

AA Auswärtiges Amt

BA-MA Bundesarchiv-Militärarchiv (Archive of the German Armed Forces)

DBFP Documents on British Foreign Policy

FRUS Foreign Relations of the United States

The Author

Stefan Scheil, *1963, studied History of the Middle Ages, Modern Times, Contemporary History, Sociology and Philosophy at the Universities of Mannheim and Karlsruhe

Magister Artium (M.A.) in 1990

Doktor der Philosophie (Dr. phil.) in 1997

Doctoral Thesis: The political Antisemitism in Germany between 1881 and 1912, (published Diss.) Berlin 1999

Current focus of research: German Antisemitism, Holocaust, International Relations in the era of the World Wars, Polish History 1919-1939 - Numerous Publications on these subjects